THE ACHE OF LOVE

WHERE THE LOVE BEGINS

SUBHAM KUMAR DHAL

I SUBHAM KUMAR DHAL, DEDICATE MY THIS VERY
POEM TO ALL THE READERS, MY PARENTS AND ALL
MY FAMILY MEMBERS ALONG WITH MY ANCESTORS.

Contents

Foreword

I AM A NEW BUDDING POET AND LOOK FORWARD FOR THE OPENION AND COMMENTS OF ALL MY READER ONES.

Preface

THIS POEM IS PURELY DRENCHED WITH LOVE THOUGHTS AND THE AUTHOR REQUESTS ALL THE READERS TO DRENCH WITH HIS FEELINGS IN THIS POEM.

Acknowledgements

MR. SUBHAM KUMAR DHAL IS A BUDDING POET AND TRIES TO WRITE NEW POEMS UPON LIFE AND ITS BEHAVIOUR TOWARDS MANKIND. THIS IS A SMALL POEM BASED ON HIS OWN EXPERIENCE. MR. DHAL IS PERSUING HIS GRADUATION RECENTLY AND AIMS TO BE ONE OF THE RENOWED POET ONE DAY.

Prologue

LOVE IS SOMETHING WHICH BRINGS US HAPPINESS AND SOMETIMES SADNESS. BUT, ONE OF THE BEST FEELINGS OF LIFE IS A PART OF LOVE ITSELF.

BY- SUBHAM KUMAR DHAL

1. THE ACHE OF LOVE

When I start expressing my love,

You are my mio amore,

My happiness,

My ache,

My shine and gain.

You are all the

Tangibles and intangibles,

I compose within me.

Whenever I miss you,

My heart merely hugs you tight.

And for your love,

I will fight

Until the last breath.

At the end,

Gathering some confidence ,

To say you about my heart's message.

But, have no guts to say…..

Authors Request

MR. DHAL WANTS TO BRING TO THE NOTICE TO ALL THAT ALL THE READERS ARE KINDLY REQUIRED TO COMMENT ON HIS OWN WRITTEN POEM.

PLEASE

HAPPY READING

THANK YOU

SUBHAM KUMAR DHAL